CLAUI

CW00819117

On

Finding Ease

in Difficult

Times

a little guide to
navigating difficult things

Borage Star Publishing
1309 Coffeen Avenue STE 1200
Sheridan, WY 82801
info@boragestarpublishing.com

Ordering Information:
Quantity sales. Special discounts are available on quantity purchases by corporations, associations, and others. For details, contact sales@borage-starpublishing.com.

On Finding Ease in Difficult Times/Claudia Olivié. —1st ed.
ISBN 978-1-7354721-0-2 (paperback)
ISBN 978-1-7354721-1-9 (ebook)

Edited by Andrew Fox
Cover Image by Sven Scheuermeier on Unsplash
Design and Layout by Lucy Giller

Disclaimer
The information in this book is not a substitute for professional medical or psychological care. If you need physical, mental, or emotional support, please see a medical or mental health professional.

If you're thinking about harming yourself, please visit crisistextline.org or text HOME to 741741 (USA) / 85258 (UK) /50808 (Ireland) to speak with a trained counselor, 24 hours a day, 7 days a week.

Dedication
• • • • • • • •

For you, dear reader.

May you experience more ease in the midst of
what you're going through,
may you know you're not alone,
and may you feel deeply loved and supported.

Contents

······

Introduction
··········

Welcome. I'm so glad you're here reading this.

Sometimes life is hard. While we often don't know *how* or *when* difficult things will show up in our lives, we *do* know that they *will* show up. It's an inevitable part of life.

Difficult things weave their way in and out of our lives over and over again, and we each end up finding our own ways of holding on when things get tough.

I wrote these notes as I navigated several difficult things in my life and struggled to stay afloat.

The intention of this book is to offer what has helped me find my own paths to ease in the midst of difficult periods in my life, as a way to help you find your own ways to more ease in the midst of difficult periods in your life – no matter what that looks like.

Since you've picked up this book, you're likely dealing with something difficult. It doesn't matter if what you're navigating are day-to-day challenges and frustrations, big life-changing turbulent times, or anywhere in between. This book is for you. I hope it helps you find your path through.

You may be wondering how to get the most out of this book. My recommendation is to trust your inner guidance. If you want to read from front to back, that's great. If you want to skip around, that's great. If you just want to let the book fall open to a page, that's great too. Trust your internal wisdom.

This book certainly isn't prescriptive. I'm sharing these notes with the intention that they help point you in the direction of your own inner wisdom and your own pathway to greater ease in the midst of any difficulty.

There's no right or wrong. There's no one thing that's right for everyone. I encourage you to try things on, and take what works for you, leaving behind what doesn't.

As you explore and try things on, it can help to remember that you don't need to decide right now if you'll hold on to any of these things for the rest of your life. You can try them on for a bit. See what happens. See what's possible for you. See how you feel. Then maybe try them on for a little while longer, continuing to check in with yourself and your own experience.

As you probably already know, there is no magic pill. But it does seem to me that finding more ease in the midst of difficult things is a skill we can cultivate. And while that's no magic pill, developing that skill can help us navigate the choppy waters of life when they inevitably show up.

My hope is that some of these notes help you find your own way through difficult times in your life. We need you. And we need you in good shape. Finding more ease in the midst of difficult things can help with that.

There is no hierarchy of difficulties

All of us experience difficulties of different kinds and different sizes.

In my own life, like so many others:

I've lived with anxiety and depression from an early age.

I've dealt with debilitating and chronic illnesses, with sometimes very frightening symptoms and difficult treatments.

I've sat with chronic pain and the despair of a body and mind that are unable to function as they used to.

I've lived out of a car and gone hungry, struggling to pay the most basic bills.

I've sat in the dark depths of grief, pain, and uncertainty.

I've navigated the mind-bending mazes of betrayal, deception, and abuse.

I've been overwhelmed, saddened, and outraged by abuses of power and injustices in the world around me.

I've also sat with things that can sometimes seem relatively minor but still create a great deal of suffering: the day-to-day frustrations, annoyances, discomforts, fears, uncertainties, anger, sadness, and the myriad challenges that we all navigate regularly.

That's just one snapshot from my own life. I'm not remarkable in that way. You have your own lists of difficult things you've navigated and continue to navigate. You likely share some of the experiences I've listed, and you likely have others.

One of the things I've learned over and over again is that there is no hierarchy of difficulties.

In many ways, the difference is in the amount of suffering, not the "level" of difficulty.

Anything can be more difficult or less difficult.
Anything can produce more suffering or not.
Anything can be done with more ease or less ease.

And when we're presented with difficult things in life, we can choose a great deal of how much we suffer while we're in them.

When we're in the midst of something difficult, it can feel like we have no hope of relief. We can so easily get sucked into the dark depths of suffering.

But there is always a way to find more ease, in the midst of anything. And it's a skill we can learn.

Like any new skill or any muscle that's gone unused for some time, it may not necessarily be easy at first.
It may take time and effort.
It may take practice.

But with practice, it becomes easier and easier, until it becomes easier to use this new skill than not to.

That, really, is the goal.

Not to always have ease, or to never suffer.

But to have it be easier to suffer less in the midst of difficult things. To have it be easier and more automatic for us to find more ease in any situation, than it is to create additional suffering, difficulty, or pain for ourselves.

What is ease?
·············

Ease is not the same as easy.
Ease does not mean a lack of challenge or difficulty.
Ease has more to do with not fighting the reality of what's happening in this moment.

That doesn't mean we don't work to change that reality. But if we can first allow ourselves to be with the truth of our current reality, we can empower ourselves to move forward with more ease and less added suffering.

So often we fight the reality of what's going on, and it paralyzes us. We end up creating an enormous amount of additional suffering for ourselves on top of what's already going on.

Ease includes being kinder to ourselves, being with the truth of our current circumstances, and not creating that additional suffering for ourselves.

There will be difficult things for us to deal with. There will be things for us to sort out and things for us to get through. There will be terrible things that we will need to navigate. And we can give ourselves the gift of not creating more suffering on top of that. We can give ourselves the gift of more ease in the midst of it.

Ease is not easy.

Finding more ease doesn't mean things aren't still hard. It doesn't mean we won't still have the wind knocked out of us. Or fall to our knees.

It simply means, that in the end, we are kinder to ourselves. We stop piling on so much unnecessary pain and suffering, and we understand that just because something is difficult doesn't mean we need to add to our suffering.

Not making it harder than it needs to be

Even in the midst of the most difficult things, we can stop making it harder than it has to be. So much of our time worrying, fretting, and planning ends up just making things harder than they already are.

Finding ease in difficult times involves some surrender, a letting go of trying to figure everything out, a letting go of trying to control it all.

Our attempts to figure everything out, to create plans, and to be strategic, they're all just ways we try to control what's happening. If we're looking for more ease in difficult times, then we're going to have to give up some of that micro-level control.

When we're trying to control all of the details, we end up distressed, anxious, and running around trying to manage all of the things.

By doing our best to let go of our need and desire to control and micromanage the difficult things in our lives, we can stop making the situation harder than it is. We can stop making it harder than it has to be.

Dropping into ease
· · · · · · · · · · · · · · · · · · ·

As we sit in the difficult times in our lives, we can create tiny moments of ease for ourselves by dropping into ease. But what does that even mean?

In this moment, can you pause, and simply sit in one moment of grace? Can you simply sit in one moment of ease?

Maybe for a few seconds. Or a single second. Or even a fraction of a second.

Can you create the tiniest moment of ease for yourself, in this moment, right now?

Can you step away from what's happening, stop all the doing, and simply *be* for one moment?

However tiny, however short, however fleeting that moment is, each time we can pause and drop into a moment of ease, we're building that muscle for ourselves.

We can continue to create these moments of ease, no matter how small, as often as we need. We can even string together a series of those moments.

By practicing sitting in a moment of ease, however small, whenever we think of it, whenever we can, soon it becomes easier and easier to drop into moments of ease. After a while, it can even become like muscle memory. It can become the thing we automatically do in those moments when we're struggling.

The more often we practice it, the more we will know deep in our bones that we can always find refuge there - without needing our environment or our circumstances to be different than they are. It's a place we can always turn to in the midst of any difficult thing. It's something we always carry with us. And we can walk through our life knowing, and trusting, that we can always find a moment of ease in the midst of anything.

Suffering now to prepare for future suffering

• • • • • • • • • • • • • • •

So much of our suffering comes from our anxiety, worry, and uncertainty about what's to come.

We try to predict the future so we can get ahead of it.

We try to predict adversity and potential future suffering so we can avoid it.

While that can make sense in terms of planning and tangibly preparing for things, we often take it one step farther. We often equate it with some belief that preemptively suffering now over something that might happen in the future will have us suffer less overall.

We can often operate from this misguided belief that we can somehow prevent ourselves from feeling sadness, anger, or pain in the future by feeling it now. Almost as if, by suffering now, we can guard against future suffering.

More often, we just create additional, unnecessary, suffering for ourselves.

It's ok to experience pain

Difficult things are an inevitable part of life. There are times when we will experience pain, sadness, upset, anger, fear, heartbreak, grief, and so much more.

Finding ease in the midst of something difficult doesn't mean that we pretend it's not happening or push those feelings down. It means that we feel what's genuinely true for us in that moment – but without adding too much to our story about it.

Creating stories is a natural thing for us to do. But the more we add to the story of why we're upset, or angry, or sad, the more we add to our suffering.

It can be hard to catch ourselves creating stories in the moment. Often we don't even realize we're caught up in a story we've created. We're so stuck inside of it.

But when we do catch it, when we do realize that we've added to our suffering through the story we've created, we can allow ourselves to question the story. We can take an honest look at what's real and what isn't; what we know to be true and what we don't.

We can release the story we created in our minds about whatever is going on, even for a moment, easing the added suffering we've dumped on ourselves.

Releasing the story doesn't mean that we don't experience the truth of our feelings. It can take time and practice to discern the truth of a situation and the truth of our feelings from the story we've made up about them.

Truly experiencing the feelings we have in a moment when we're going through something difficult is helpful. It's important to feel what's true for us in those moments. And at the same time, we can avoid ruminating on it.

We can allow those feelings to flow through us, allow ourselves to feel them to whatever extent we can in that moment, and then allow them to pass, without adding more to them by creating a story about why we feel them and what it means. We can feel it all and then see what the next moment brings.

We can be in pain and not suffer
••••••••••••••••••••••••••••••••••

As odd as it may sound, we can be in any experience and not suffer.

We can feel cold and not suffer. We can feel hot and not suffer. We can experience discomfort and not suffer. We can be tired and not suffer. We can be in pain and not suffer. We can even experience intense pain and not suffer.

We can experience the sensations and not necessarily experience suffering.

The suffering comes from our fighting against what's happening, from our need for it to not be happening, or for things to be different. The suffering comes from our desire to not be feeling what we're feeling; to not be experiencing what we're experiencing.

Can we, just in this moment, accept the conditions we're in right now? Can we, just in this moment, accept the situation we're in, the sensations we're experiencing, without needing it to be different or needing it to not be happening?

That doesn't mean we don't also act when appropriate. But, even then, we can act from a place of clarity and acceptance of the truth of the current situation, without additional suffering on top of it.

Like clouds
....

There's an important distinction between allowing ourselves to feel the feelings we have when we're going through something difficult, and ruminating on, or clinging to, those feelings.

If we find ourselves holding on to our feelings, ruminating on them or building a story around them, we end up adding to our suffering in that moment.

Instead, we can let the feelings flow through, experience them fully, and then let them pass, much like clouds in the sky.

Sometimes clouds pass quickly with minimal effect other than creating a temporary shadow. It might feel a little cooler while the cloud's overhead, but then it passes and we're back to what was there before.

Sometimes the clouds last longer, and have a greater effect – like rain clouds. They could cause a light sprinkling or a downpour. But given time, those clouds pass too.

Like clouds, sometimes the intense feelings we experience pass quickly with minimal effect and afterwards things are as they were before.

Sometimes, we'll feel them for longer. They may come and go in waves, and they may have bigger, or even lasting, effects. We may see things differently or change our actions in some way, or others may change their perceptions or actions towards us. But once the cloud passes, it's time to deal with whatever's in front of us now, rather than clinging to the cloud.

If we hang onto it, or if we add stories about the past or future, we're no longer letting the cloud pass overhead. We're now pulling it back and adding to our suffering.

Instead, we can try to simply be present for the cloud. Witness it. Allow it to be. Let it move through and pass without attaching other things to it. Without clinging to it, or adding a story to it.

Then, once the cloud, or the intense feeling, passes, we can assess what's going on in that moment. We can assess our external and internal environment, as well as our state of mind. We can gauge what's most needed now, and what action would serve us best, in this moment. And then we can begin it.

The action could be small, like resting, asking for help, or doing some small task. Or it may be big. It could even be something simple like a conversation. What's most helpful is to stop and decide what the best course of action is now, in this moment, at this particular point in time, knowing the next moment may bring something new.

It's ok to be at peace

Sometimes we make things so much harder than they need to be. Sometimes we have a belief that the difficult things we're dealing with must also be hard, and then we make them harder. We make them more difficult than they need to be.

Know that we can rest in the midst of it. We can be at peace in the midst of it.

Even though we may be going through something difficult, we don't need to suffer, and we certainly don't need to create additional suffering for ourselves.

Sometimes we may feel or think that it's our job to suffer. That suffering is required. Well-meaning people may even reinforce that by telling us how much we must be suffering, or acting as if we're wrong if we're not actively suffering in that moment. But that's just a story. It's not truth.

The truth is that we don't need to suffer simply because something's difficult.

That's not to say we'll never experience suffering. We will. And that's ok. That's part of being human. But we don't need to suffer, or add to our suffering, for the sake of it, or because we think we're supposed to. We don't need to make things more difficult for ourselves out of this idea that it's supposed to be difficult.

There's space for kindness towards ourselves, space for ease, and even space for play in the midst of any difficult thing we're dealing with. And it's ok to be in those spaces too.

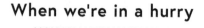

When we're in a hurry
••••••••••••••••••••••

Often, we're in a hurry to release, or get rid of our pain. We become focused on making the painful moment end as quickly as possible. But, often, that just creates more pain and more suffering.

Instead, we can catch ourselves in those moments and try to simply allow the pain to be, without being in a rush to get rid of it.

We can sit with it in that moment, like sitting with a small child or a dear friend who's struggling. We can simply allow space for it. Letting it be, instead of trying to force it out.

Pain and suffering are not bad, in and of themselves. They simply *are*.

When we attach labels to them, or when we make ourselves wrong for feeling them, we end up piling more pain and suffering on top of what's already there.

The more we pull away, the tighter its grip. But if we can catch ourselves and step into it instead of pulling away, if we can simply allow it to be as it is, we can release the grip of that added pain and suffering, which will ultimately have us suffer less.

A single breath
• • • • • • • • • • • • •

Breathe. Breathe fully. Breathe easily.

Even if the breath itself is hard, we can still add ease to it, by allowing it to be as it is.

Breathe in. Hold it. Breathe out. Hold it. Breathe in. Hold it. Breathe out. Hold it. Breathe in. And so on.

Each part is just as important as the last.

So often, we breathe in and hold. Or breathe out and hold. We don't complete the cycle. But our very life depends on us completing the full cycle of breath, both literally and figuratively.

Where can we add a little more ease to the next breath? Where can we do it more smoothly, softly, slowly, releasing any tension? Infusing just one breath with more ease.

If all we can manage in a day is to add ease to a single breath, that's something. We still will have found some ease in that day.

Some days are tough. Some days will knock us to the ground. Some days will shake us to our core. And even on those days, we can find some ease. Even if it's just in a single breath.

Every bit counts. Each act of rest, each act of ease, counts. It all adds up. So often we forget that. It all counts. It all matters. It all contributes. This breath, in this moment, counts.

The ripple effects of a single moment of ease can spread far and wide. This one moment with even just a touch more ease will affect all the moments that come after it, which will all affect the moments after that.

Each time we bring a tiny bit of ease to a moment, whether through our breath or something else, we affect every moment of our life that comes after.

Each moment, each breath, each time we bring more ease to our lives, affects everything else. No act of ease or rest is too small to make a difference.

In each moment we can begin again
....

In each moment, we can begin again.

Each second, each nanosecond, is new, and holds the possibility of a fresh start, to begin again, to start over.

So often, we're fighting against ourselves. We may think we *should* suffer, or we *should* feel guilty. Or we may catch ourselves suffering, and then we fight *that*, thinking that we shouldn't be suffering, that we know better, or that someone else has it worse.

In either case, we're adding to our suffering by fighting ourselves.

Instead of fighting ourselves, we can begin anew right now. In this very moment. We can ask: Am I ok in this moment? Is there anything that I need in this moment? We can drop the internal commentary like the heavy weight that it so often is.

We can always pick it back up again if we find we need to, or want to. We don't need to give it up forever. We can simply see if, in this moment, it's possible to do without it. Even if just for a moment.

Sometimes we may only be able to experience it moment by moment. That's ok. Practice allows us to build the muscle, and as the muscle gets stronger, it becomes more natural and normal.

Whenever we remember (or even at preset times during the day), we can check in, see if we're suffering unnecessarily, and drop it, even temporarily. Let it go, temporarily. See who we are without it, temporarily.

We don't need to permanently give up anything. And right now, just for a moment, can we suspend our conviction that we must suffer, allow ourselves to feel what life is like without that winter coat. We may end up surprised by what we find out.

When we feel alone
····················

Sometimes, when we're sad or going through a difficult time, other people shy away, or are afraid of us, or have certain expectations about us. People may avoid us, or be hesitant to be around us, hesitant to say something. That can leave us feeling alone and isolated.

In those moments, we're never truly alone. We are always supported. It can help to remember all of the other beings surrounding us in this moment, and all the ways we're supported by everything around us.

Right now, inside of us are trillions of bacteria – trillions of organisms that are always with us.

All around us are insects, various animals, plants, fungi, other human beings.

And beyond the living beings and organisms, we can look to the atoms and the particles all around us. We are constantly impacting – and being impacted by – all of the particles around us. We are always part of a larger conversation, part of a larger ecosystem.

The trees, the wind, the clouds, the water, the blades of grass, the flowers, the rocks, the air, the soil, the sunshine, the rain, the snow, the falling leaves, the insects – they are all in conversation with us. There is a constant dance going on between all of us.

Even beyond what's physically around us, there are so many memories we hold inside of us. Those memories of our loved ones are also with us, and we can play those memories in our minds at any time. We can be with them at any time.

In so many ways, we are never truly alone. If we can take a moment to truly notice all of the life, all of the beings, all of the particles, and the memories that are here with us right now, we would know we are not alone. We are never alone. Even if it sometimes feels like it.

When we're drowning in overwhelm

Sometimes it can feel like we're so overwhelmed that we're drowning. It's hard to take even the smallest step forward.

That's ok too.

Even the smallest shift will have ripple effects. We can begin wherever we are, wherever we can. The tiniest change is enough to cause a chain reaction that makes future shifts easier.

Making simple, tiny shifts, as tiny as can be, as often as we're able to, will add up.

One place we can begin is with the small things that we can do for ourselves in that moment. What small act of kindness, care, or compassion can we give ourselves? Maybe it's taking a nap or visiting with a friend. Maybe it's taking a bath or going outside.

Later on, when we feel well enough, we can even make a list of things that can help us in those moments – like an emergency self-care list. Then when we're feeling overwhelmed, we can just review the list we already made for ourselves, and pick one tiny thing that feels doable in that moment.

There is no right or wrong way
....

There is no right or wrong way to do life. There is no right or wrong way to be upset. There is no right or wrong way to be happy. There is no right or wrong way to be sad. There is no right or wrong way to feel ease. There is no right or wrong way to experience anything. We simply experience as we experience.

That doesn't mean we can't change our perspective, or that we can't change our experience through internal shifts, or even through external actions.

But there is no right or wrong when it comes to our experience.

Often, we make ourselves wrong for what we're feeling and experiencing. We think we should be joyful when really we're devastated. We think we should be "over it" and back to normal, when really we're outraged. Sometimes we even feel a need to undo our happiness, or feel guilty about our happiness, if something difficult is happening as well. Like they can't exist in the same space.

We block ourselves every which way because we think we're somehow doing it wrong.

There is no right or wrong way to experience your life and what you're going through.

Choosing again in each moment

There is no peace outside of us. The experience of peace and greater ease comes from within us.

In any circumstance, we can choose to experience peace or not. We can choose to experience greater suffering, or we can choose to ease our suffering. We can choose our perspective in each moment.

That's not to say there aren't difficult things, or that we will never suffer. But in each moment, even in the midst of difficult things, in the midst of suffering, we can choose ways of being kinder to ourselves.

Each moment presents that opportunity all over again. It's not as if we choose once and that's it, or we now have to sit and wait around for another opportunity. Each moment, each millisecond, presents a new opportunity to *choose again*. There's always a new opportunity to choose to a new perspective, to choose to ease our suffering, to choose to be kinder to ourselves.

We get to choose our perspective moment to moment. We won't

always consciously choose it. That's ok. We're human. But whenever we notice it, we can make a new conscious choice.

The more often we notice and consciously choose, the easier it becomes. It becomes easier for us to notice, which means it becomes easier for us to see new opportunities to choose, all of which opens us up to more opportunities for ease.

Then, over time, we can start to create a new mental pattern, like a groove in our brain that's so well worn that it becomes the easiest route. Until it becomes our habitual pattern, and we don't even need to consciously choose to change our perspective as often – it naturally happens more often.

That's one of the greatest benefits of consistently noticing and *choosing again*, as often as we can.

There will, of course, be times when we miss opportunities to choose. That's ok. We're human. And again, even in those moments when we notice, we can simply *choose again*, right then and there. Rather than being upset with ourselves, we can choose to be kinder to ourselves, to notice it and continue on.

Treating heartbreak like physical breaks
....

When our heart is broken, healing it can involve many of the same things as healing a broken bone.

If we break our leg or our arm, we stop. We rest. We don't harm it further. We're more careful with it. We dote on it. We care for it. We take more time with it. We stop doing things that make it hurt. We do less.

The same things are helpful for heartbreak. Stopping. Resting. Not doing things that hurt or harm our hearts more. Taking more care. Taking more time. Doing less.

So often we forget to take care of our hearts when they're broken. We don't stop. We don't rest. We don't take sufficient care. Instead, we often harm our hearts more, by being frustrated that it's not already healed, or exposing ourselves to things that cause us more pain. That doesn't help heal a broken heart any more than it helps heal a broken bone.

Finding ease, not creating ease

Finding ease.

Not creating ease.
Not making ease.
Not transforming into ease.

FINDING ease. Discovering it. Uncovering it. As it appears naturally.

In many ways, it's a treasure hunt. We can look for those small moments, those tiny moments of peace, ease, and joy, in the midst of the difficulties.

Sometimes that means, as it naturally happens, we notice it. Sometimes it means more actively looking for it in any moment.

At any given moment, we may only be able to do one or the other. That's ok. Either is helpful. Either is good. We're not "doing better" at finding ease when we're actively seeking it out. Simply noticing where it naturally happens is enough. If we can just notice a moment of ease, any moment of ease, that is a victory.

In either case, we're focusing on finding the ease that is already there, rather than trying to create it.

We also don't need to notice ALL the moments of ease.

Sometimes we play these games with ourselves, berating ourselves for not finding every possible moment of ease.

Instead, we can focus on cherishing our ability to find whatever moment of ease we do find. Whether it's right at that moment, an hour later, a day later, or a week later. We do not need to "excel" at finding ease. We do not need to "work" at finding ease.

Finding ease doesn't mean pushing, pulling, or trying to force anything. It's about uncovering what's already there.

We don't need to create it. It's already there. We can just notice and drop into it whenever we're able.

We are always supported
·····························

We are supported in this moment.

Whatever we're sitting, standing, or lying on right now, it's supporting us.

The particles underneath us are pushing up against the particles that make up our bodies, and the particles that make up our bodies are pushing down on the particles of what's underneath us. It's this beautiful partnership dance of just enough force to support us in this moment.

All of the particles that surround us in this moment, surrounding every inch of our skin, hair, and clothing, they are all supporting us. The air around us is supporting us in our breathing. Each particle around us, is in some way interacting with us, and supporting us.

The lines of where one thing begins and another ends are not as clear as they look. There are no lines delineating where there are and aren't particles. There are particles everywhere.

There are no delineations of "something" and "not something".

The air around us is filled with particles, in the same way we are filled with particles. What we're resting on is filled with particles, in the same way we are. Every other person, every other being, every object, is filled with particles just as we are.

Like one of those dot paintings where we can see the figures when we look at it from farther away, but when we look up close, there's no clear delineation – one thing blurs into the next. We are made of particles, and everything around us is made up of particles, and those particles are all supporting us in some way. We're in a constant dance with all of it.

It's not a betrayal

When we're in the midst of a difficult period, as we have moments of feeling better, we may find ourselves starting to look for the suffering. As if it's a betrayal to experience these moments ease, happiness, calm, or normalcy in the middle of the difficult things we're going through.

So often, we are our own biggest barriers to experiencing more ease in the midst of something difficult. We don't allow ourselves to experience these oases of ease, these oases of happiness, of calm, of normalcy. We feel guilty or wrong. We feel as if we're betraying someone or something.

It's not a betrayal to feel ease. It's not a betrayal to feel happy. It's not a betrayal to feel calm, to feel better, to feel normal, in the midst of these difficult things.

Sitting with our pain
• •

When we're experiencing pain, whether physical, mental, or emotional, it often serves as a messenger for us.

The pain becomes sharper as we try to ignore it, and lessens as we begin to listen. It may continue to poke and prod at us until we acknowledge it, sit with, listen to it.

Rather than trying to ignore or dull the pain, we can do our best to welcome it. To allow it to be there with us. The way we might invite a small child into our laps, and hear what they have to say, we can welcome the pain, sit with it, and hear what it has to say.

It will pass

········

When we're in the midst of our pain, we can think that it will last forever. It can feel as if it will never end, as if it will always be this painful.

The more we can remember that everything changes, the more we can soften our grip and see beyond the pain we're experiencing in this moment. And that itself can give us a moment of relief.

Even if we focus on just this one moment in front of us right now. Everything about this moment will pass. Everything about this moment will change.

It can be hard for us to believe that when we're stuck in our pain. We may not be able to see it. We may be so stuck in our minds and in our pain. But we can do our best to focus on what's right in front of us. Simply making it through this day. Or this hour. These next few minutes.

These moments will pass, just like every other. Our experience will change, just like everything else. It will change. It will pass. As much as it seems like it won't, it will. It always does.

Oases in the midst of difficult times

Each moment has its own signature. Even in the midst of difficult times, there will also be moments of joy, love, laughter, ease, and peace.

Often we focus so much on the difficult moments that we forget to pay attention to this moment that's in front of us now, in all its glory.

Just like each child is different, with their own way of being, their own personality, and their experiences, each moment is different too.

Imposing the feelings of the last moment on this one has us miss out on the opportunity to embrace the beauty of this new moment.

Even in the midst of these difficult times, there is beauty, happiness, joy, and laughter. We may not always feel them, but we can notice little glimpses of them – like spotting an oasis in the distance.

We can pay attention to them. We can stop letting them pass without noticing. And most importantly, we can enjoy them, even savoring them, without feeling guilty about it.

So often we pass by one of these mini-oases without stopping. Because we think we don't deserve it, or we think we shouldn't experience happiness or ease when we're in the middle of these difficult things. But we can stop, and it's not only ok to stop, it's both good and needed.

When we find ourselves laughing in the midst of our grief, when we find ourselves relaxing and feeling at peace in the midst of a very tumultuous or stressful time, when we find ourselves hopeful or inspired in the midst of uncertainty, that is beautiful and good. That is something for us to enjoy and savor. We can use these oases to rest, to recover, to replenish ourselves for the next leg of the journey ahead.

By bringing our attention to them, by stopping and resting there, the oases grow and multiply, so that we end up with more oases where we can rest, recover, and be replenished along the way during this difficult period in our lives.

Trusting ourselves
·················

There are times when we can feel bombarded by well-meaning people in our lives who tell us what we "should" or "shouldn't" be experiencing, feeling, or doing.

It can be helpful to remember that no one else can truly know what's best for us. We have spent many more hours on this planet understanding ourselves, understanding what we need and don't need; experimenting with what works for us and what doesn't. Our knowledge and experience of ourselves is much greater than any other being on this planet.

In the end, while we can seek counsel and advice, particularly from trusted sources, in the end, we must trust ourselves.

We have far more information about ourselves than anyone else in the world. We know our strengths, our weaknesses, our history, our current experience, our capacities in any given moment.

How does a tree find ease?

Trees can serve as beautiful examples of finding ease.

The tree stands in its place, firm in its roots, allowing other things to move around it, and moving with them as much as needed.

The tree's core, its trunk, supports the rest of the tree. It stands still, firm, unwavering, and calm.

The branches grow, shift, and change year to year. Sometimes they drop off or break. Sometimes they regrow, or grow in new directions. The branches move as needed with the wind, with animals walking on them, with the heaviness of fruit. The branches are visibly affected by the changing environment.

The roots grow underground, seeking out what the tree needs to grow and stand firm. The roots are what first build that steady, firm foundation, and they are what support the growth of the branches and all of the outcroppings.

If we look at ourselves as a tree, so often we focus on our branches — those parts that are interacting most visibly with the changing environment and circumstances. We don't realize we first need a steady trunk and healthy roots seeking out what we most need. Without that steady trunk and healthy roots, the branches and all of the outcroppings can't grow and be supported.

In difficult times a branch may break off. A new branch may grow in its place. Or not. Either way, if the trunk and the roots are still intact, the tree survives.

That's true of us in difficult times too. Difficult periods in our lives may alter our branches, but our trunk can remain steady throughout. Then, to grow a new branch, our roots can seek out what we need.

As winter approaches, a tree's leaves may change color and then fall to the ground. The tree doesn't mourn the loss of its leaves. It sheds them as it prepares for the winter that's coming. It doesn't try to grow new branches or new leaves during that time. It focuses on stabilizing itself for the difficult winter. It takes care of its core needs.

Then as the warmer weather approaches, the tree grows again. It grows its roots, it grows its branches, it grows new leaves, and it grows flowers and fruit.

It doesn't hold onto its experience of winter and continue to hunker down even after the winter has passed. It doesn't get upset when the next winter approaches. It moves with, and adjusts to, the changing circumstances as best it can.

So often, as we enter difficult periods in our lives, we can resist letting go of the things we need to let go of in those moments. We desperately cling to them, leaving ourselves weaker and not taking care of our core needs.

And then as the difficult period passes, we can find ourselves clinging to that too, holding on and hunkering down, leaving us stuck in it even after it's over. We begin fearing and resisting the difficult things that may be ahead of us, and not caring for ourselves, instead of moving with the changing circumstances as best we can.

Growth comes from ease
· ·

We often think that growth comes from the difficulty and the pain. Those may spur the impetus for growth, but the actual growth happens in the midst of ease.

If we look at a plant, for it to grow, it needs a quiet time or space in which to grow, and its basic needs must be met. If it's constantly bombarded and never gets a break from defending itself or protecting itself, it can't grow.

The growth might be triggered by a lack of something, or a need to get something it doesn't have, but the actual growth itself must happen in the midst of some ease.

The same is true of a muscle. If we're physically training, we're testing our muscles and putting them through difficult circumstances. That triggers a need to grow. But the growth itself happens during a period of rest, of ease.

The same is true for us on the whole. While it can be helpful to embrace the challenges and difficulties in life, to truly grow with them, we need to embrace the ease and the rest as well.

Ease is always there
· · · · · · · · · · · · · · · · · · · ·

Ease is available in any moment. It's always there, ready to be found.

Like a body of water, there might be chaos and intense movement on the surface, but there is ease underneath the surface.

Sometimes we need to dive in to find the ease, but it's always there.

Our feelings are valid
....

At times we will feel lost.
At times we will feel alone.
At times we will wonder how we will make it through this.

That's ok. It's normal.
There's nothing wrong with us for feeling that way sometimes when things are difficult.

We can notice those feelings, sit with them, and allow them to pass when they do.
All of our feelings are valid.

The pain of what if...

When we're going through something difficult, we may find ourselves wondering about if something had been different.

What if we had said or done something differently?
What if that thing hadn't happened?
What if something else had happened?

We get lost in the maze of our imaginations, wondering what would have happened if things had been different.

It's understandable.

We do it out of an instinct and desire to prevent more suffering in the future, but in the end, those questions often just create more suffering.

Our ruminating on them doesn't change the thing. It doesn't make it better. It doesn't take away our pain. Instead, it usually adds more pain and suffering on top of what we were already experiencing.

Other people
....

Sometimes other people in our lives wish to help in ways that aren't what we most need.

They may experience tension when they can't help, or feel a need to be needed, and they may try to help in ways that helps them to relieve their own tension or stress, but not necessarily in ways that are helpful to us.

Sometimes we may find ourselves needing to protect ourselves from the well-meaning people in our lives.

It can be helpful to understand where the intention is coming from, and that they're likely struggling with tension and stress in their own bodies. Understanding that can help us to release some of the anger, resentment, and frustration that can show up when someone's "help" is unhelpful to us.

Often, the thought of having a conversation about what we need and don't need can feel like an added burden that we don't have energy for. Instead, we may allow others to walk all over us. We may collapse our space. We may not tell others we need them to stop doing something.

Taking care of ourselves is most important, and sometimes that includes releasing ourselves from unnecessary suffering around misunderstandings. Sometimes, if we can see the positive intention, however misplaced, in the other person, we can have a smoother, clearer conversation that speaks to the specifics of what we need and don't need from them.

Finding ease in all times

There is a grace that happens when we know, beyond a shadow of a doubt, that we can be with anything. That we can find ease in anything.

It allows us to navigate life differently, to see things differently, to react differently, knowing that, no matter what happens, we can be with it and find ease in the midst of it.

It's a skill, and just like any other skill, it can be learned and cultivated over time. If we can find ease in difficult times, we can find ease in all times.

Grateful acknowledgments
....

This book would not have been possible without the help of so many along the way.

An enormous thank you to:

Lindsey Smith & Alexandra Franzen for sharing your knowledge and expertise, and for the endless support, encouragement, and love notes along the way.

Lucy Giller & Andrew Fox for all of your input, creativity, patience, and work in helping bring this book to life.

Graham for picking me back up when I needed it, and encouraging me to go ahead despite all my stumbling.

Derek Sundquist for your friendship and encouragement, for sharing your passion for writing with me, and for being one the most loving, kind, and amazing humans on the planet. I am so grateful to have you in my life even though I don't get to see you often enough.

BB for your connection and deep caring, for sharing what you saw in me, and allowing me to grow into that.

My jolly giant for your unwavering support and steadiness through it all.

The feral ponies of Holy Isle for allowing me to walk with you when I needed to clear my head.

And the many, many friends and loved ones who have supported and encouraged me in so many ways over the years. Your kindness has had a big impact on me.

I also want to thank all of the people who have confided in me about their own difficult times over the years – you are amazing and you inspire me daily.

About the author

························

Claudia Olivié writes and teaches on wellness and self-care, helping to guide people to their own ways of caring deeply for themselves.

She especially loves teaching people how to create a "User's Manual" for themselves, so that they (and their loved ones) know exactly what brings out the best in them, with a lot more ease – and how to troubleshoot when things go sideways.

When she's not writing and teaching, you can find her exploring new places, listening to audiobooks, or playing with whatever ingredients she has on-hand in the kitchen.

Find out more, and receive free resources, at claudiaolivie.com.

CPSIA information can be obtained
at www.ICGtesting.com
Printed in the USA
LVHW091945160920
666192LV00009B/1866

9 781735 472102